Geoff Wilson's guide to
RIGGING
BRAID, DACRON & GELSPUN
LINES

Geoff Wilson's guide to RIGGING

BRAID, DACRON & GELSPUN

LINES

Revised edition 2006
First published in 1999 by
Australian Fishing Network Pty Ltd
48 Centre Way, South Croydon, VIC 3136
Telephone: (03) 9761 4044
Facsimile: (03 9761 4055
Email: sales@afn.com.au
Website: www.afn.com.au

Copyright © Australian Fishing Network 2006

ISBN 186513 099 0

CONTENTS

INTRODUCTION

The past fifty years or so has seen the introduction of first, nylon monofilament fishing lines, and later, braided nylon and dacron fishing lines. Now, the introduction of polyethylene gelspun fishing lines, sometimes called Super Lines, gives anglers yet another option.

These lines are presented in braided and fused forms. Of the samples tested by the author, the braided lines were limp and supple like cotton while the fused lines were stiffer and somewhat easier to manage.

Gelspun fishing lines vary in quality from one brand to the next but most are very fine for their strength. In addition to being very strong, gelspun fishing lines have minimal stretch.

These properties are an advantage for skilled anglers: The fine diameter providing for increased line capacity, and the lack of stretch providing for the easier hooking of fish, and recovery of line.

For less skilled anglers, lack of stretch becomes a liability because the line that does not stretch, will not only break with little warning when too much pressure is applied—but may also contribute to the breakage of fishing rods through poor angling technique. On no account should these fine polyethylene gelspun lines be used as hand lines.

Largely because of their fine diameter, Super Lines require different knot tying and rigging strategies to either monofilament or dacron. This publication details a number of rigging strategies for Super Lines taking strength and convenience into account.

GEOFF WILSON

ABRASION RESISTANCE

Gelspun lines have sometimes been described as being more resistant to abrasion than monofilament lines. My tests indicate that of the two lines with the same diameter, one gelspun, one monofilament —each under the same load—the gelspun will resist abrasion better than the monofilament.

However, of the two lines with the same breaking strain, one monofilament, the other gelspun—each under the same load—the monofilament line will resist abrasion better than the gelspun line. This is an important consideration when choosing between gelspun and monofilament lines for fishing amongst rocks or other submerged objects.

TYING SUPER LINES TO TERMINALS

Super Lines may be tied directly to metal fittings like hooks, rings, or the towing eyes of lures provided the correct knots are used. Let's look at some of the knots used for this purpose and what percentage of the Super Lines's strength the angler can expect to retain when using that particular knot.

It is important to note that some manufacturers of Super Lines understate their products breaking strains by a wide margin. Knot strengths given are as close to a percentage of the Super Line's actual strength as I could reasonably ascertain. This means my figures for knot strengths will usually be much lower than knot strengths based on the breaking strain quoted by the manufacturer.

ATTACHING SUPER LINES TO REELS

This method of attaching gelspun lines to the spool of a reel is suggested by well known Australian angler and television presenter Peter Morse. For convenience of illustration a plain spool represents the spool of a reel in these diagrams.

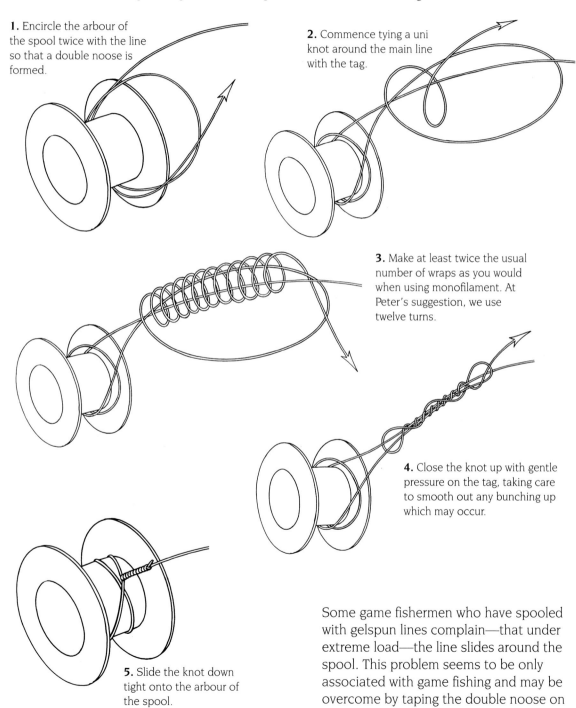

1. Encircle the arbour of the spool twice with the line so that a double noose is formed.

2. Commence tying a uni knot around the main line with the tag.

3. Make at least twice the usual number of wraps as you would when using monofilament. At Peter's suggestion, we use twelve turns.

4. Close the knot up with gentle pressure on the tag, taking care to smooth out any bunching up which may occur.

5. Slide the knot down tight onto the arbour of the spool.

Some game fishermen who have spooled with gelspun lines complain—that under extreme load—the line slides around the spool. This problem seems to be only associated with game fishing and may be overcome by taping the double noose on line firmly to the arbour of the spool.

TRIPLE PALOMAR KNOT

72%

The Triple Palomar Knot is recommended for tying Super Lines to metal rings and hooks. It never slips and retains a high percentage of the line's breaking strain.

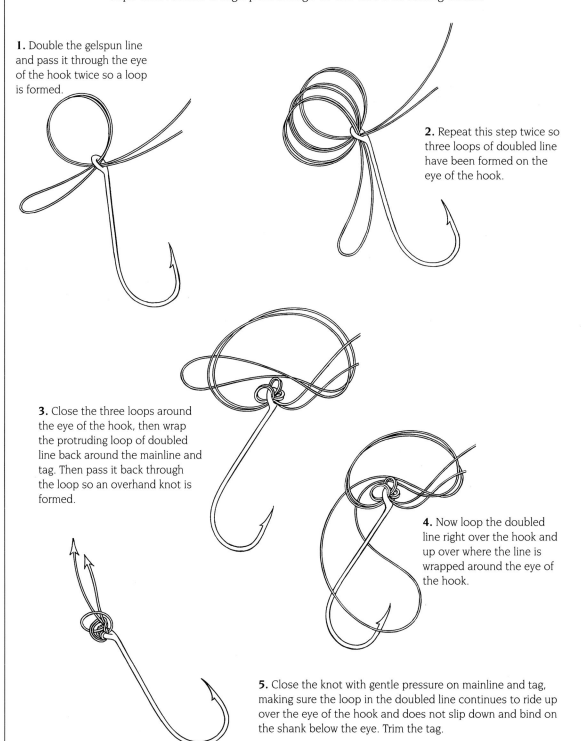

1. Double the gelspun line and pass it through the eye of the hook twice so a loop is formed.

2. Repeat this step twice so three loops of doubled line have been formed on the eye of the hook.

3. Close the three loops around the eye of the hook, then wrap the protruding loop of doubled line back around the mainline and tag. Then pass it back through the loop so an overhand knot is formed.

4. Now loop the doubled line right over the hook and up over where the line is wrapped around the eye of the hook.

5. Close the knot with gentle pressure on mainline and tag, making sure the loop in the doubled line continues to ride up over the eye of the hook and does not slip down and bind on the shank below the eye. Trim the tag.

BRAID RING KNOT

65%

The Braid Ring Knot provides a secure connection for hooks, rings and swivels.

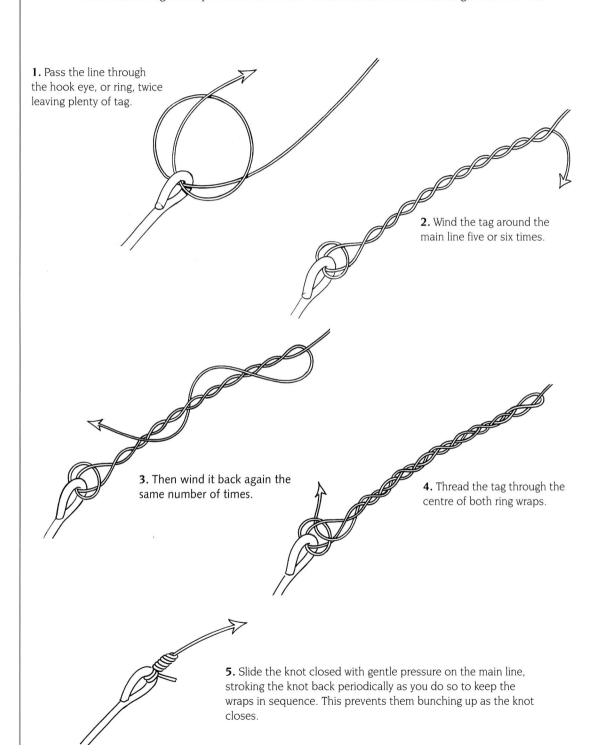

1. Pass the line through the hook eye, or ring, twice leaving plenty of tag.

2. Wind the tag around the main line five or six times.

3. Then wind it back again the same number of times.

4. Thread the tag through the centre of both ring wraps.

5. Slide the knot closed with gentle pressure on the main line, stroking the knot back periodically as you do so to keep the wraps in sequence. This prevents them bunching up as the knot closes.

BRAID SNELL

92%

This is the strongest method I have discovered for attaching a hook directly to any Super Line.

1. Hold the hook with the eye to the left and the bend to the right. Extend a 30 centimetre (one foot) tag and wrap it around the shank of the hook in an anti-clockwise direction as shown.

2. Having completed a spiral of five or six turns, commence a tight binding back in the opposite direction.

3. Keep the wraps as close as you possibly can, and continue binding almost, but not quite, up to the eye of the hook.

4. Now turn the hook around. Fold back the tag so a loop is formed, and finish the binding clockwise.

5. Rotating the loop as shown, over-bind the tag all the way up to the eye of the hook. Should you have difficulty doing this, chances are you commenced binding in the opposite direction than what was indicated.

6. Close the remaining loop by pulling out the tag.

7. Shown is the finished snell with the tag trimmed short.

The main line emerges from the snell a short distance back from the eye of the hook, although not as far back as it appears to be in this diagram due to the exaggerated thickness of the line.

SILLY SNELL

80%

One of the easiest of all hook attachments, it retains 80% of any Super Line's breaking strain when tied correctly. This is more than adequate for almost any fishing situation. However, it should not be used with extremely fine lines that may jam between eye and shank of the hook.

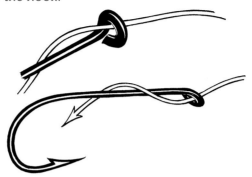

1. Thread the eye of the hook and wrap the line around the shank, taking care you wrap away from the end of the wire which has been rolled to form the eye of the hook: This is most important.

2. Begin wrapping back up the shank of the hook with the tag.

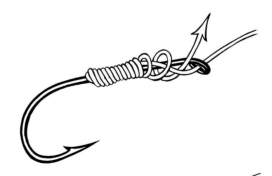

3. Continue almost back to the eye of the hook so that you have a binding some 1.5 cm (5/8") long. Then, simply tuck the tag under the last wrap as shown.

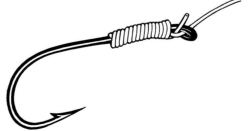

4. Slide the wraps up to the eye of the hook, pulling on the line to tighten the snell.

COLLAR AND CAPSTAN

78%

This knot was developed for tying fine gelspun lines directly to the towing eye of a lure.

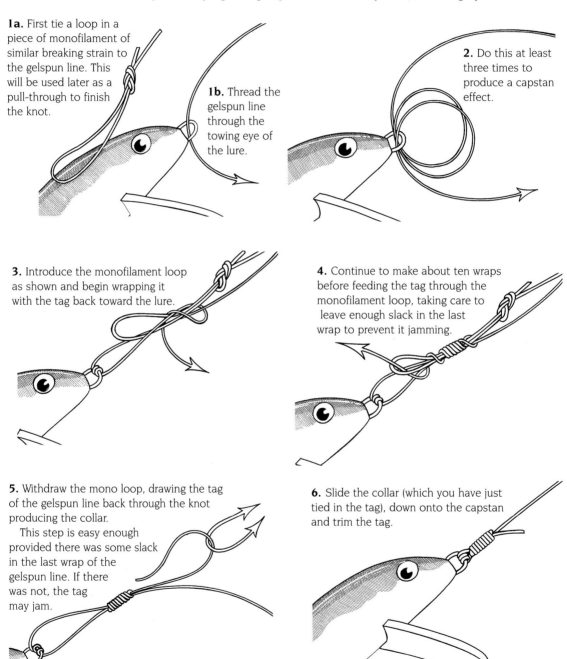

1a. First tie a loop in a piece of monofilament of similar breaking strain to the gelspun line. This will be used later as a pull-through to finish the knot.

1b. Thread the gelspun line through the towing eye of the lure.

2. Do this at least three times to produce a capstan effect.

3. Introduce the monofilament loop as shown and begin wrapping it with the tag back toward the lure.

4. Continue to make about ten wraps before feeding the tag through the monofilament loop, taking care to leave enough slack in the last wrap to prevent it jamming.

5. Withdraw the mono loop, drawing the tag of the gelspun line back through the knot producing the collar.
   This step is easy enough provided there was some slack in the last wrap of the gelspun line. If there was not, the tag may jam.

6. Slide the collar (which you have just tied in the tag), down onto the capstan and trim the tag.

Tested on 24 lb Spiderwire Fusion, (which actually tested over 25 lbs), the Collar and Capstan broke at 22 lbs (88%) against the Braid Ring Knot and Triple Palomar at 19.6 lbs. In braided lines it tested, on average, around 78%.

TWISTED LEADER KNOT FOR ATTACHING A MONOFILAMENT LEADER

60%

This is one of the strongest methods I know of tying a single strand of gelspun line to a monofilament leader. I tested it six times with a sample of Berkley Fireline which was labelled 14 pounds (probable breaking strain 30 pounds). When tied to a 12.5 kg Maxima monofilament leader, the highest test obtained was 9.4 kg (20.7 pounds). Only one knot tested below 8 kg (17.6 pounds).

1. Wind the gelspun line (black) around one end of the monofilament leader. I suggest doing this twenty times.

2. Form a knot in the twisted lines and pull the entire monofilament leader through.

3. Do the same again so another wrap is added.

4. Do this two more times so four wraps are made.

5. Then, with firm but gentle pressure on all four legs, close the knot.

Should a loop of slack gelspun line appear within the knot as it closes, release the mono leader tag and apply tension to the gelspun line until the loop disappears.

6. Close the knot firmly and trim the tags.

MONOFILAMENT PATERNOSTER

30%

This very popular, bottom fishing rig, makes use of a monofilament hook and sinker leader. It is used for catching fish which usually weigh a good deal less than the breaking strain of the line being used to catch them.

I first tested it by tying a sample of Berkley Fireline marked 14 lbs to various monofilament leaders testing from 4 kg (8.8 lbs) to 13.6 kg (30 lbs), with an Albright knot. The Albright knot broke at 4 kg consistently, which was about 62% of my Fireline sample's stated breaking strain, or about 30% of its actual breaking strain, as near as I could determine.

This knot was then tied in 20 pound Berkley Gorilla Braid and again tested at 4 kg. 45% of the line's stated breaking strain or 35% of the line's actual breaking strain which was 11.4 kg, as near as I could determine.

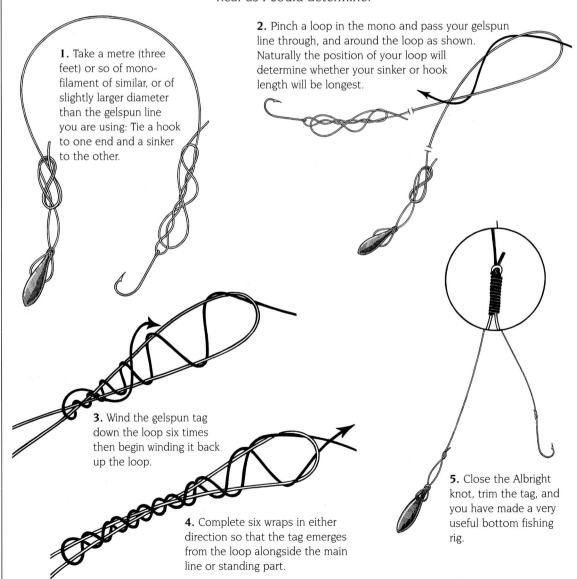

1. Take a metre (three feet) or so of mono-filament of similar, or of slightly larger diameter than the gelspun line you are using: Tie a hook to one end and a sinker to the other.

2. Pinch a loop in the mono and pass your gelspun line through, and around the loop as shown. Naturally the position of your loop will determine whether your sinker or hook length will be longest.

3. Wind the gelspun tag down the loop six times then begin winding it back up the loop.

4. Complete six wraps in either direction so that the tag emerges from the loop alongside the main line or standing part.

5. Close the Albright knot, trim the tag, and you have made a very useful bottom fishing rig.

PATERNOSTER OR FIXED SINKER RIG

This rig is not recommended for general use because it is inclined to tangle. However, I have used it successfully when fishing for whiting in the surf with Berkley Fireline which is quite a bit stiffer than the braids and therefore less likely to tangle.

1. Take first step is to tie a short Bimini Double in the end of the Super Line. But, first mark the main line or standing part to which the hook is usually tied.

2. Tie your Bimini and cut the loop so that two separate strands are formed.

Naturally, you can make split terminals with other loops like the Surgeons Loop, but—although the Bimini takes longer to tie—it is the best choice when maximum strength is required.

3. Attach a hook to the marked leg using one of the knots recommended for that purpose, then tie a sinker to the other leg using a simple loop attachment.

4. Tie an overhand loop in the other end and attach your sinker.

RUNNING SINKER RIG IN SUPER LINE

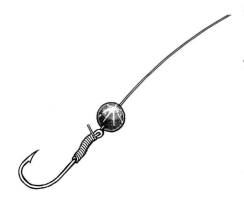

Shown here is a simple rig exploiting the unobtrusive nature of gelspun fishing line. The hook is simply tied directly onto the end of the line using a snell. The ball sinker shown in this diagram is added, either to give the rig added weight for longer casts, or to anchor the bait in a tidal stream.

When larger ball sinkers, or smaller hooks are used, it is a good idea to thread a small plastic or rubber bead, like a lumo bead, onto the line to prevent the eye of the hook jamming in the hole through the sinker.

RIGGING WITH SUPER LINES FOR MAXIMUM STRENGTH

Loop-to-loop connections are widely used for attaching wind on leaders for sport and game fishing, and—in fly fishing—for attaching a fly line to the backing on the reel.
The Bimini Twist is the most satisfactory method I know for producing a strong double or end loop in gelspun line.

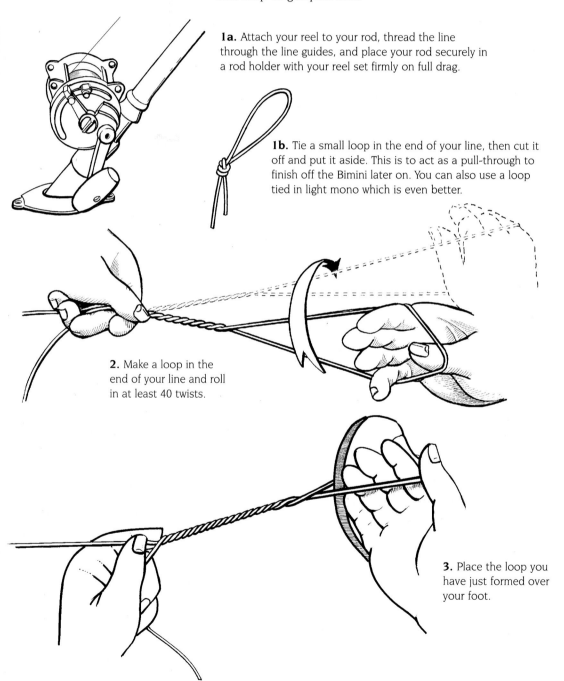

1a. Attach your reel to your rod, thread the line through the line guides, and place your rod securely in a rod holder with your reel set firmly on full drag.

1b. Tie a small loop in the end of your line, then cut it off and put it aside. This is to act as a pull-through to finish off the Bimini later on. You can also use a loop tied in light mono which is even better.

2. Make a loop in the end of your line and roll in at least 40 twists.

3. Place the loop you have just formed over your foot.

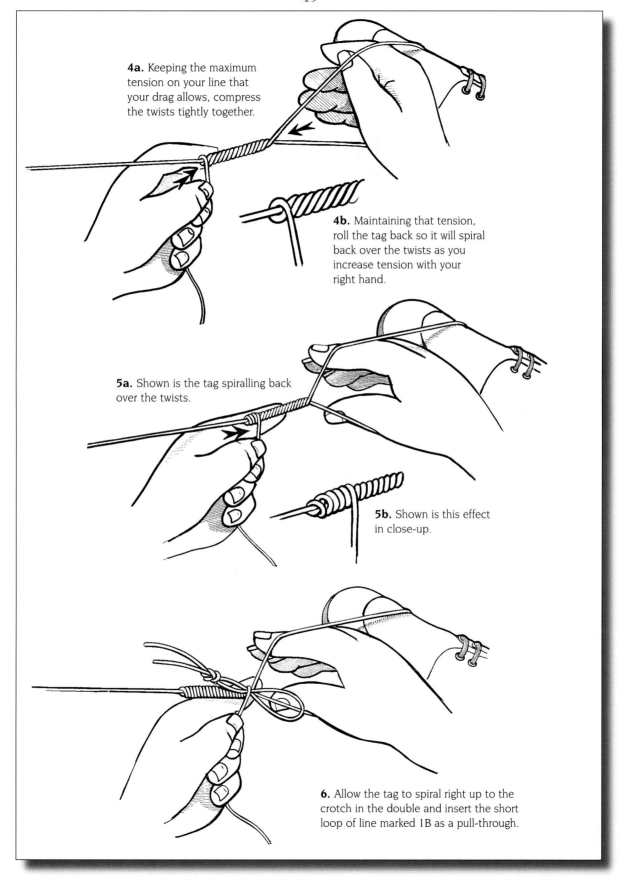

4a. Keeping the maximum tension on your line that your drag allows, compress the twists tightly together.

4b. Maintaining that tension, roll the tag back so it will spiral back over the twists as you increase tension with your right hand.

5a. Shown is the tag spiralling back over the twists.

5b. Shown is this effect in close-up.

6. Allow the tag to spiral right up to the crotch in the double and insert the short loop of line marked 1B as a pull-through.

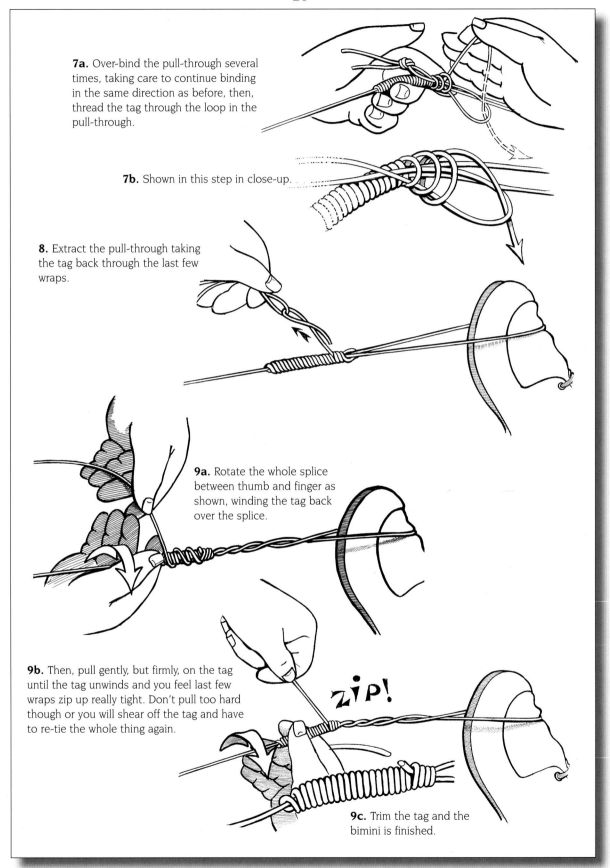

7a. Over-bind the pull-through several times, taking care to continue binding in the same direction as before, then, thread the tag through the loop in the pull-through.

7b. Shown in this step in close-up.

8. Extract the pull-through taking the tag back through the last few wraps.

9a. Rotate the whole splice between thumb and finger as shown, winding the tag back over the splice.

9b. Then, pull gently, but firmly, on the tag until the tag unwinds and you feel last few wraps zip up really tight. Don't pull too hard though or you will shear off the tag and have to re-tie the whole thing again.

zip!

9c. Trim the tag and the bimini is finished.

JOINING SUPER LINES WITH THE BIMINI CATS PAW SPLICE 88%

Tied in twelve different lines, this join between two gelspun lines retained, on average, 88.25% of the tested breaking strain, by far the strongest join between two gelspun lines that I have tested. Four of the lines tested reached 100% of the tested breaking strain.

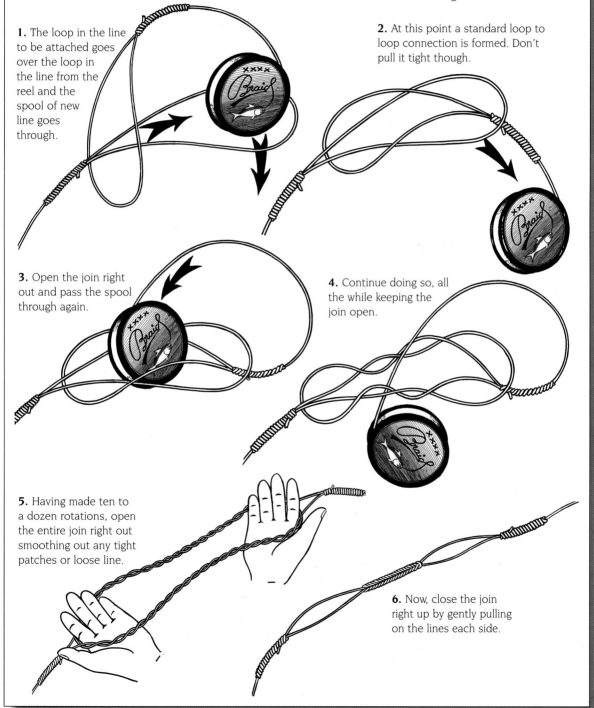

1. The loop in the line to be attached goes over the loop in the line from the reel and the spool of new line goes through.

2. At this point a standard loop to loop connection is formed. Don't pull it tight though.

3. Open the join right out and pass the spool through again.

4. Continue doing so, all the while keeping the join open.

5. Having made ten to a dozen rotations, open the entire join right out smoothing out any tight patches or loose line.

6. Now, close the join right up by gently pulling on the lines each side.

LOOP & CROSS-LOOP

This version of the loop to loop connection is used and recommended by leading salt water fly fisherman Rod Harrison for joining gelspun backing to the spliced loop at the end of a flyline. The loop in the gelspun backing is achieved using the Bimini Twist. Doubling the loop to produce two strands instead of one—a preferred strategy—may be achieved by first doubling the gelspun line before tying the Bimini, tying a second Bimini with the doubled strand, or by tying a surgeons loop.

For clarity of illustration, the loop spliced in the end of the flyline is larger that it would normally be, and the flyline dispenser reduced in size and simplified.

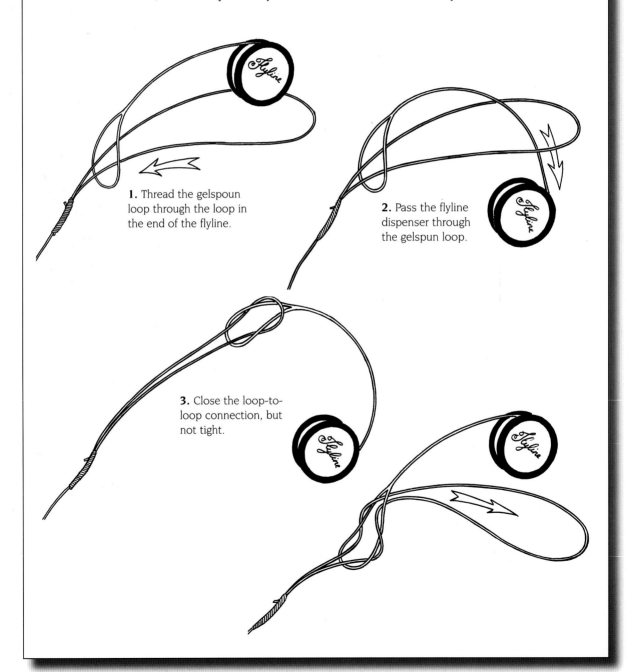

1. Thread the gelspoun loop through the loop in the end of the flyline.

2. Pass the flyline dispenser through the gelspun loop.

3. Close the loop-to-loop connection, but not tight.

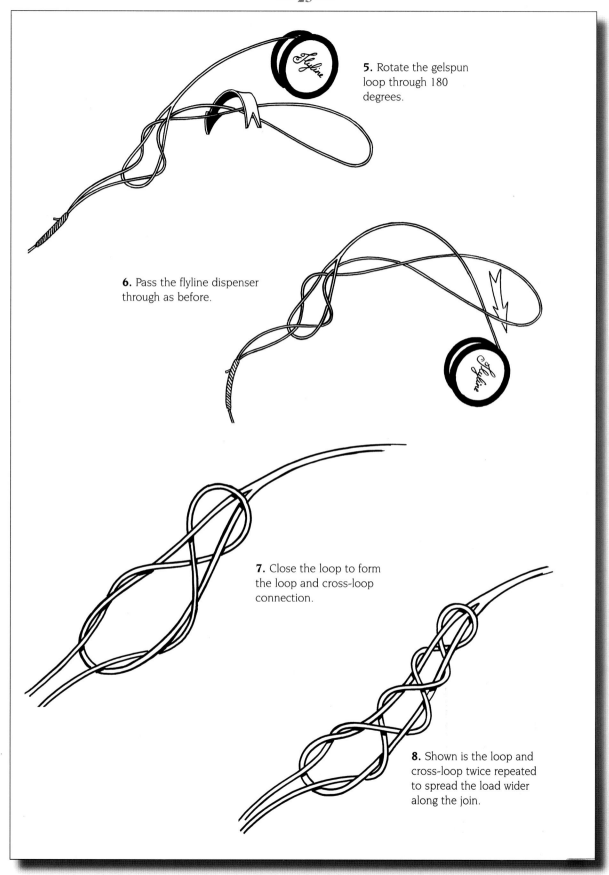

5. Rotate the gelspun loop through 180 degrees.

6. Pass the flyline dispenser through as before.

7. Close the loop to form the loop and cross-loop connection.

8. Shown is the loop and cross-loop twice repeated to spread the load wider along the join.

ATTACHING MONOFILAMENT LEADERS TO SUPER LINES

A most useful strategy when fishing with Super Lines is to attach an extended monofilament leader, long enough to be wound onto the reel. This allows all terminal rigging to be done with the monofilament.

One method of attaching a monofilament leader to a Super Line is with a Braid Leader Knot.

STEPS IN TYING THE BRAID LEADER KNOT

1. Wind the Bimini Double around the monofilament leader working away from one end.

2. When using monofilament of the same breaking strain as the Super Line, I recommend you make ten wraps with the Bimini Loop, then—wind the tag of the monofilament leader back around those, effectively making at least one more additional wrap which makes the next step easier. When using a monofilament leader with a breaking strain substantially above the breaking strain of the Super Line, you will find it necessary to reduce the number of wraps so the knot can be tightened.

3. Holding onto the mono tag, with your finger in the crotch of the loop and tag, pull gently bit firmly until, One; the loop of the Bimini Double reduces in size, and two; the mono tag binds firmly around the wraps you made in the Super Line. Then, you can release the tag and close the knot with firm pressure each side.

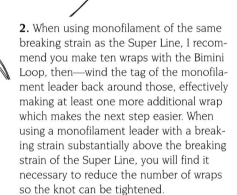

4. The finished knot should look like this.

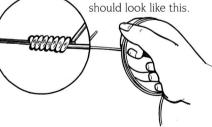

5. This variation of the Braid Leader Knot is used when the Bimini Double has been cut or broken, but remains long enough to be tied. Both strands of the Super Line double are laid out straight, then tied together with a simple overhand knot. Then a uni knot or grinner is tied around the monofilament leader.

The uni knot is then closed up tight and the stiffer monofilament leader is then wound back around the Super Line double the required number of times before the monofilament tag is passed through the first wrap, between monofilament and Super Line, alongside the uni knot. The knot is then closed by applying pressure on the line each side.

GAME FISHING RIGS

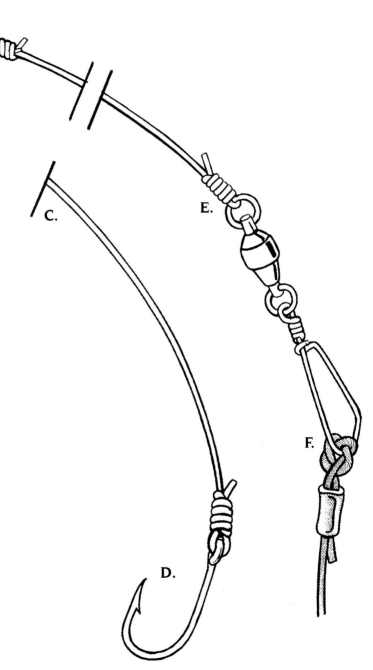
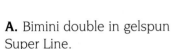

A. Bimini double in gelspun Super Line.

B. Gelspun double joined to monofilament leader with a Braid Leader Knot. (Naturally the Braid Leader Knot is replaced with a Dacron Leader Splice when using roller guides.)

C. Monofilament leaders used in game-fishing are usually four to nine metres in length and twice to four times the breaking strain of the main line.

D. A simple rig for strip-baiting in a berley trail for tuna.

E. Another simple rig terminating in a snap-swivel allowing wire traces and the like to be added easily.

F. A snap-swivel at the end of the monofilament leader permits pre-rigged leaders to be changed easily.

DEEP SEA BOTTOM RIGS

FOR BLUE EYE TREVALLA ETC

A. Bimini double in gelspun line.

B. Double in gelspun line

C. Braid leader knot joining gelspun line to monofilament leader.

D. Monofilament leader at least four metres long.

E. Twisted dropper loop in monofilament leader to prevent tangles when deep-dropping.

F. Heavy sinker attached with a loop.

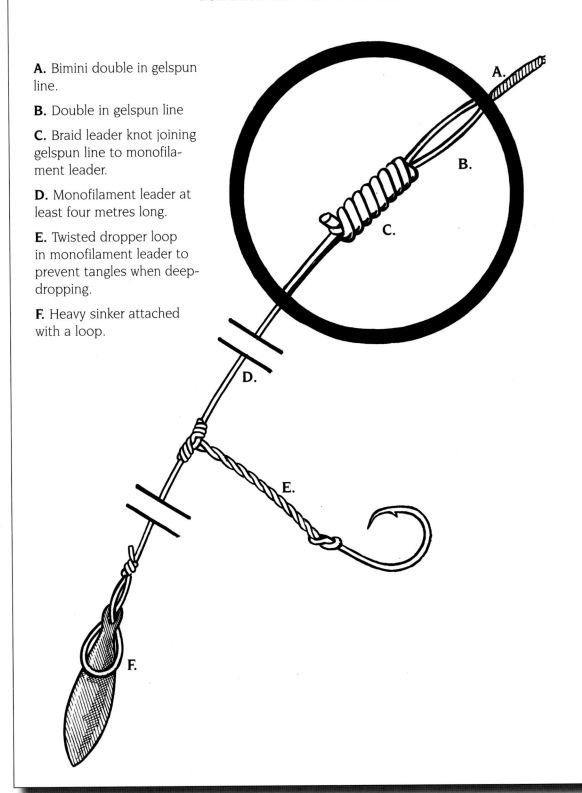

TED DONELAN'S LEADER CONNECTION

While other connections in this book are designed for attaching somewhat heavy monofilament leaders to lighter gelspun lines, this one – shown to me by veterinary surgeon and keen angler Ted Donelan – is best suited for attaching relatively light monofilament leaders. It passes easily though the rod guides when either casting or retrieving and retains the full strength of the gelspun line

1. Having spliced an end loop in your gelspun line with a Bimini Twist, take a severed length of monofilament leader, fold one end into a loop and pass the gelspun loop through.

2. First wrap one leg of the gelspun loop with the doubled leader, pulling the entire length of the leader through,

3. Then wrap the other leg, and so on.

4. Continue until four to eight complete wraps are made, the greater the difference in diameter between the two lines, the fewer the number of wraps that are required, and vice versa.

5. Tension the join, first with equal pressure on both legs of the leader against the gelspun line, then on the main or standing part of the leader only.

6. When the join has been pulled up as tight as it will go, then cut off the tag.

MIKE CONNOLLY'S LEADER KNOT

57%

Tested in three lines, 14 lb Spiderwire Fusion, 30 lb Spiderwire, and 30 lb Fins PRT Braid, this leader knot tested, on average 98.3% of the stated breaking strains of those lines, and 57% of the tested breaking strains.

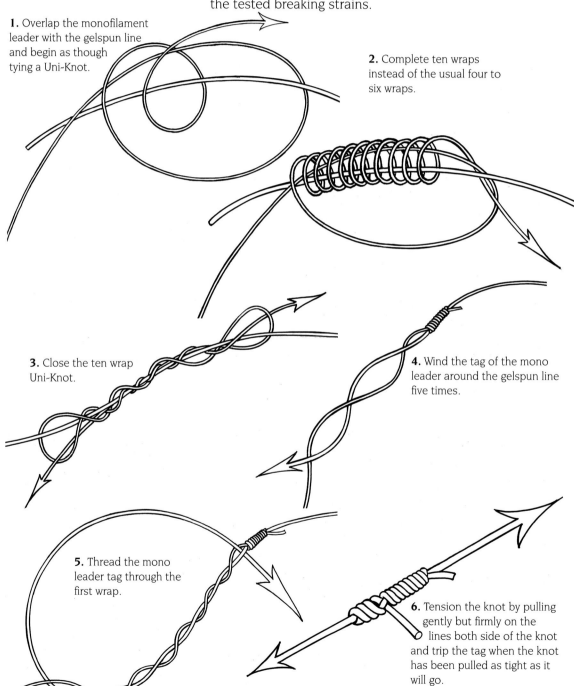

1. Overlap the monofilament leader with the gelspun line and begin as though tying a Uni-Knot.

2. Complete ten wraps instead of the usual four to six wraps.

3. Close the ten wrap Uni-Knot.

4. Wind the tag of the mono leader around the gelspun line five times.

5. Thread the mono leader tag through the first wrap.

6. Tension the knot by pulling gently but firmly on the lines both side of the knot and trip the tag when the knot has been pulled as tight as it will go.

NAIL KNOT
LEADER CONNECTION

74%

This join was tied in three lines, 14 lb Spiderwire Fusion, 30 lb Fins PRT Braid and 20 lb Cortland Spectron, connecting each to a length of 60 lb monofilament. On average, the knots broke at 136% of the line's stated breaking strains and 74% of their tested breaking strains.
To tie this knot you will need a slim metal tube like the Lumbar puncture I used and which is available from surgical suppliers. Commercially available nail knotting tools are far too coarse for fine gelspun lines.

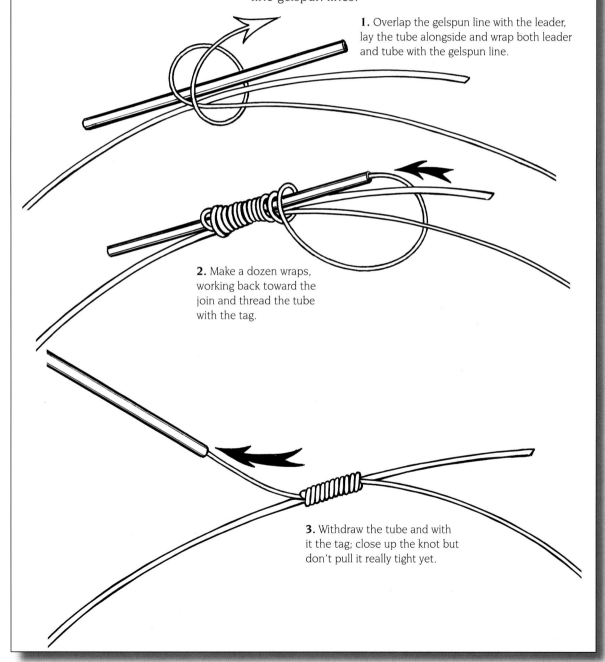

1. Overlap the gelspun line with the leader, lay the tube alongside and wrap both leader and tube with the gelspun line.

2. Make a dozen wraps, working back toward the join and thread the tube with the tag.

3. Withdraw the tube and with it the tag; close up the knot but don't pull it really tight yet.

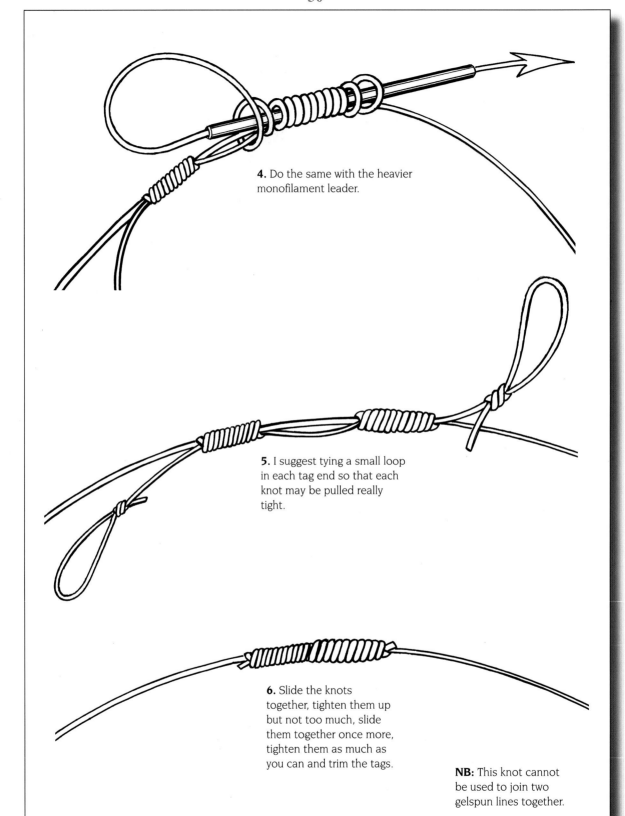

4. Do the same with the heavier monofilament leader.

5. I suggest tying a small loop in each tag end so that each knot may be pulled really tight.

6. Slide the knots together, tighten them up but not too much, slide them together once more, tighten them as much as you can and trim the tags.

NB: This knot cannot be used to join two gelspun lines together.

NAIL KNOTTING LEADER TO DOUBLE

This is a particularly effective method of attaching a twisted monofilament double, or gelspun double, to a heavier monofilament leader. You will need a rigid tube of suitable diameter to tie this knot.

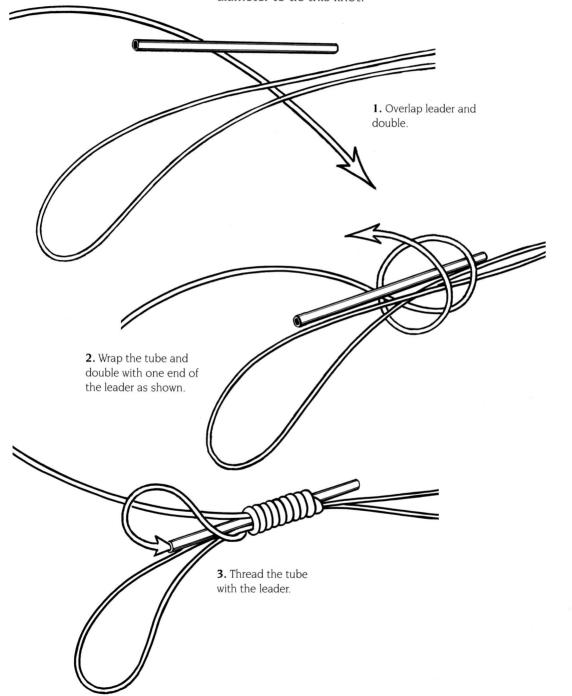

1. Overlap leader and double.

2. Wrap the tube and double with one end of the leader as shown.

3. Thread the tube with the leader.

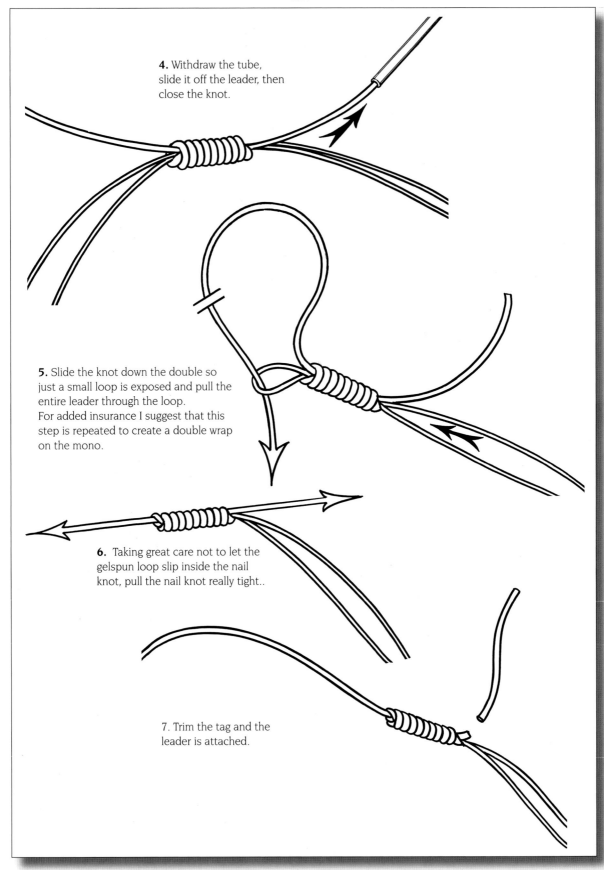

4. Withdraw the tube, slide it off the leader, then close the knot.

5. Slide the knot down the double so just a small loop is exposed and pull the entire leader through the loop.
For added insurance I suggest that this step is repeated to create a double wrap on the mono.

6. Taking great care not to let the gelspun loop slip inside the nail knot, pull the nail knot really tight..

7. Trim the tag and the leader is attached.

JOINING GELSPUN LINES WITH DOUBLE UNI KNOT

50%

The double Uni Knot has become a firm favourite for joining gelspun lines of similar or different breaking strains. On a good day it will retain 50% of the lighter line's true breaking strain if tied with the additional wraps required.

I specify true breaking strain, because the strength designation on some gelspun lines indicates a much lower breaking strain, sometimes less than half, of what testing indicates.

This fact is responsible for some for some erroneously quoting breaking strains as high as 100% for this knot, when controlled testing usually indicates about half that figure.

Some advocate doubling the line before tying this knot. However, unless the doubled line has been secured with a Bimini or other progressive splice to form a secure loop, there is little, if any, advantage in doing so.

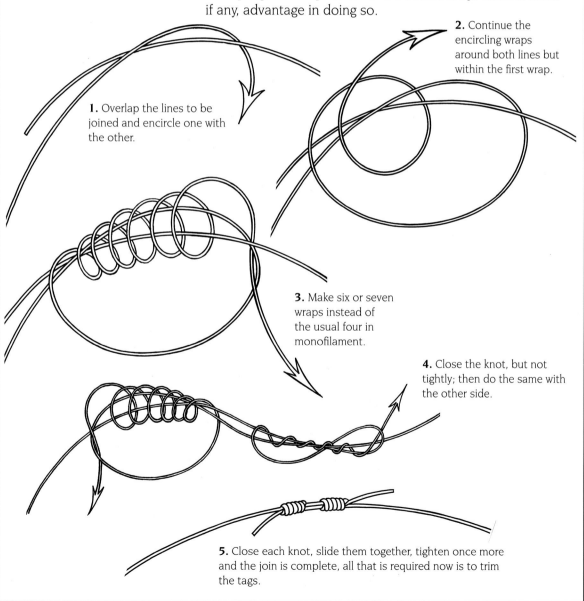

1. Overlap the lines to be joined and encircle one with the other.

2. Continue the encircling wraps around both lines but within the first wrap.

3. Make six or seven wraps instead of the usual four in monofilament.

4. Close the knot, but not tightly; then do the same with the other side.

5. Close each knot, slide them together, tighten once more and the join is complete, all that is required now is to trim the tags.

RIGGING WIND ON LEADERS FOR EXTENDED CASTS, OR FOR GAME FISHING

Unfortunately, leader knots may disintergrate if they pass through level-winds on reels, or the line guides on rods, at the very high speeds reached when making extended casts from the beach, or with heavy lures. Also, when using roller guides, the leader knot may stick to the guides.

These problems are solved by loop splicing a length of heavy gelspun line, then sliding it over the end of the monofilament leader from which it cannot be pulled off. This same splicing technique has long been used with hollow dacron lines and butt leader material like Gudebrods.

TOP SHOT WIND-ON LEADER

This wind-on leader splice was created by Steve Morris of Top Shot Tackle Australia. It is best performed using Top Shot dacron splicing needles and loop guage. Top Shot glues have been formulated for tacking dacron to monofilament, but suitable alternatives include Aquaseal and Pliobond.

Additional material include a 50 cm length of hollow braid. Several metres of heavy monofilament trace and some waxed thread.

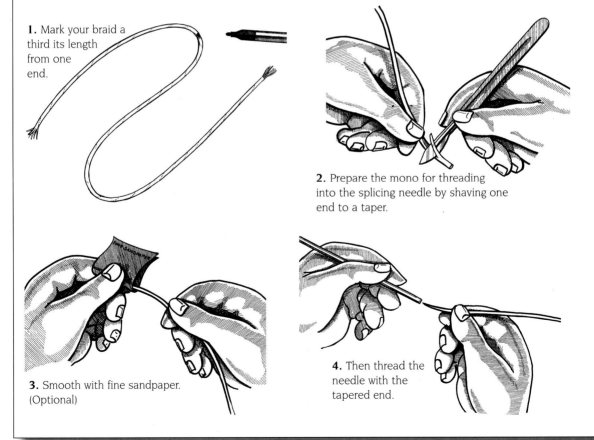

1. Mark your braid a third its length from one end.

2. Prepare the mono for threading into the splicing needle by shaving one end to a taper.

3. Smooth with fine sandpaper. (Optional)

4. Then thread the needle with the tapered end.

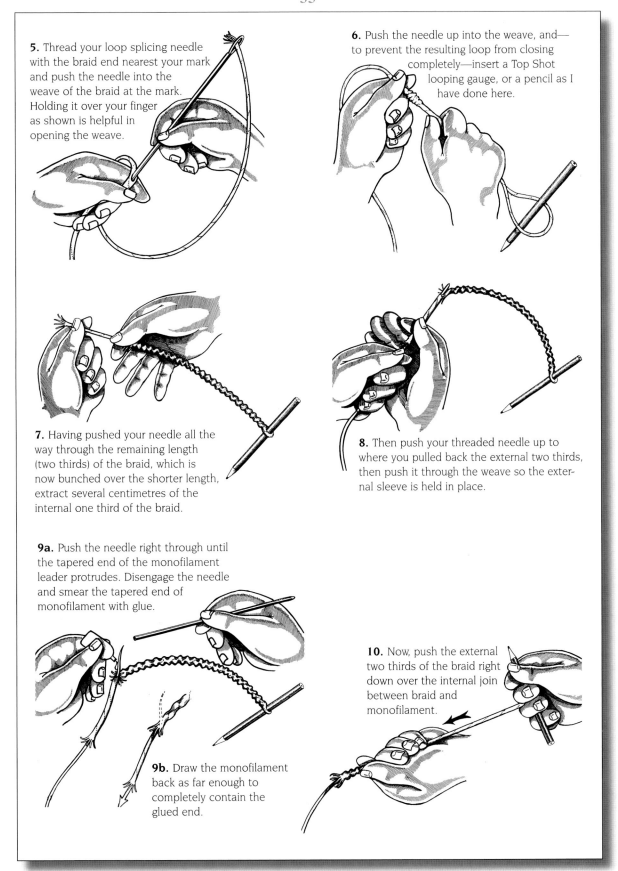

5. Thread your loop splicing needle with the braid end nearest your mark and push the needle into the weave of the braid at the mark. Holding it over your finger as shown is helpful in opening the weave.

6. Push the needle up into the weave, and—to prevent the resulting loop from closing completely—insert a Top Shot looping gauge, or a pencil as I have done here.

7. Having pushed your needle all the way through the remaining length (two thirds) of the braid, which is now bunched over the shorter length, extract several centimetres of the internal one third of the braid.

8. Then push your threaded needle up to where you pulled back the external two thirds, then push it through the weave so the external sleeve is held in place.

9a. Push the needle right through until the tapered end of the monofilament leader protrudes. Disengage the needle and smear the tapered end of monofilament with glue.

9b. Draw the monofilament back as far enough to completely contain the glued end.

10. Now, push the external two thirds of the braid right down over the internal join between braid and monofilament.

11a. Pull the braid end back a bit and smear the monofilament with glue at this point.

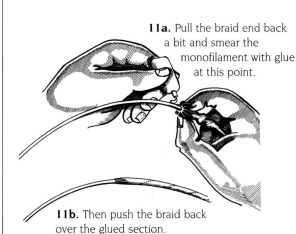

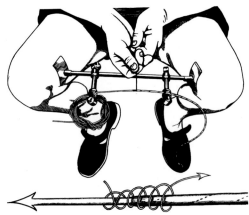

11b. Then push the braid back over the glued section.

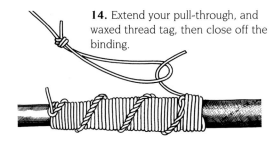

12. Stretch the leader out tight using either a Top Shot spreader, or other suitable means.
Then with your waxed thread, make a hitch on the monofilament just below the braid to secure it. Then make a series of half hitches back up the monofilament and back over the dacron edge.

13. Continue thus until the waxed thread binding extends a similar distance each side of the end. Then, over-bind a loop of thread which you can use as a pull-through to finish off your binding.

14. Extend your pull-through, and waxed thread tag, then close off the binding.

15. The finished splice should look like this representation and pass easily through the line guides of your rod when joined to a short double in your main line with a loop to loop connection or 'Cat's Paw'.

Use at least one coat of waterproof sealant like Aquaseal or Pliobond and allow to cure.

TWO HOOK RIG ON HEAVY GELSPUN OR DACRON LEADER

This method of rigging two hooks on a heavy gelspun trace or leader was devised by Steve Morris of Top Shot Tackle Australia.
It is also suitable for use with either hollow dacron or butt leader material like Gudebrods.
For best results a Top Shot dacron splicing needle is required.

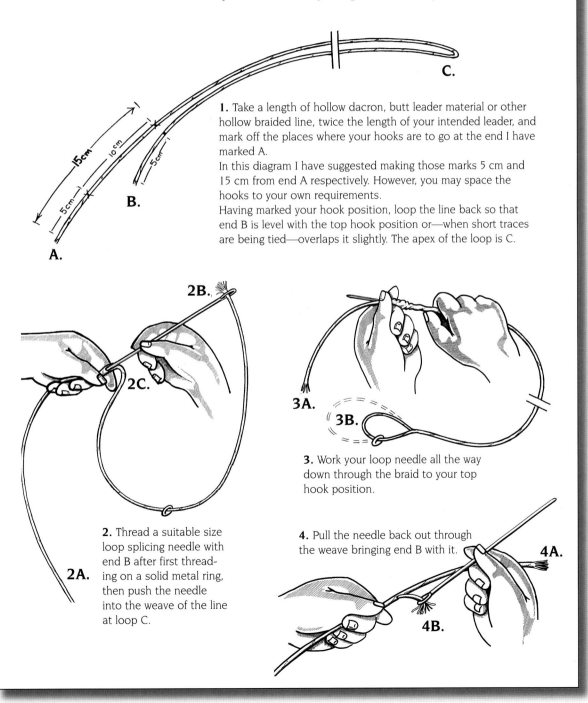

1. Take a length of hollow dacron, butt leader material or other hollow braided line, twice the length of your intended leader, and mark off the places where your hooks are to go at the end I have marked A.

In this diagram I have suggested making those marks 5 cm and 15 cm from end A respectively. However, you may space the hooks to your own requirements.

Having marked your hook position, loop the line back so that end B is level with the top hook position or—when short traces are being tied—overlaps it slightly. The apex of the loop is C.

2. Thread a suitable size loop splicing needle with end B after first threading on a solid metal ring, then push the needle into the weave of the line at loop C.

3. Work your loop needle all the way down through the braid to your top hook position.

4. Pull the needle back out through the weave bringing end B with it.

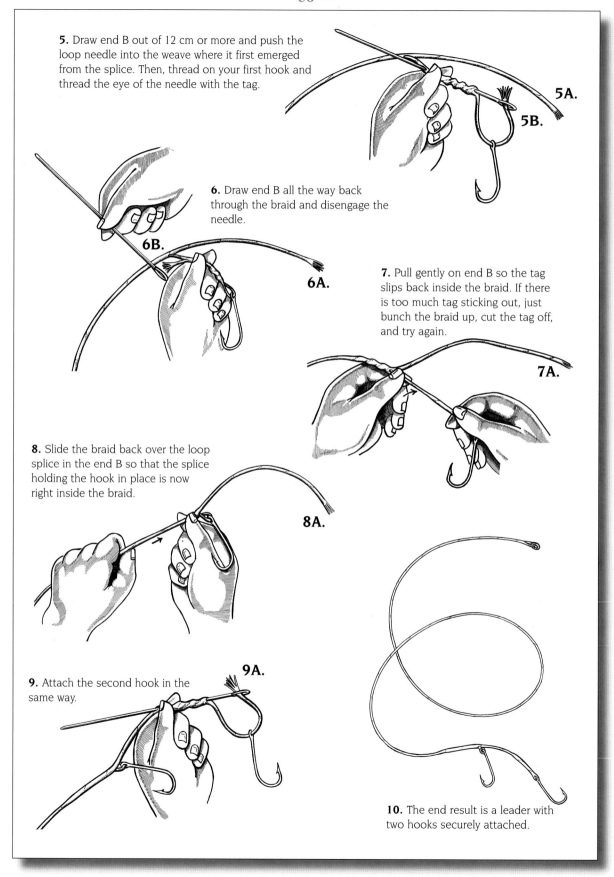

5. Draw end B out of 12 cm or more and push the loop needle into the weave where it first emerged from the splice. Then, thread on your first hook and thread the eye of the needle with the tag.

5A.

5B.

6. Draw end B all the way back through the braid and disengage the needle.

6B.

6A.

7. Pull gently on end B so the tag slips back inside the braid. If there is too much tag sticking out, just bunch the braid up, cut the tag off, and try again.

7A.

8. Slide the braid back over the loop splice in the end B so that the splice holding the hook in place is now right inside the braid.

8A.

9. Attach the second hook in the same way.

9A.

10. The end result is a leader with two hooks securely attached.

TOP SHOT DACRON JOINING SPLICE

This method of jpoining two lengths of IGFA, line class dacron, is used and recommended by Steve Morris of Top Shot Tackle in South Australia. A Dacron splicing needle is required.

1. Overlap the lines to be joined by a generous margin, say 60 cm or two feet. We will call the dark coloured line B, the light coloured line A.

2. Thread your dacron splicing needle with end of A. Then, some 50 cm from the end of B, insert your dacron splicing needle, pass it through the dacron for about 10 cm or 4 inches, and push it out again.

3. Pull the end of A out through B.

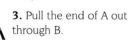

4. Straighten out B, trim the tag of A, and test join by pulling A against B as shown.

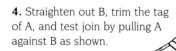

5. Thread your dacron splicing needle with the tag of B and pass the needle through A, right up close to where it emerges from A.

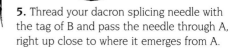

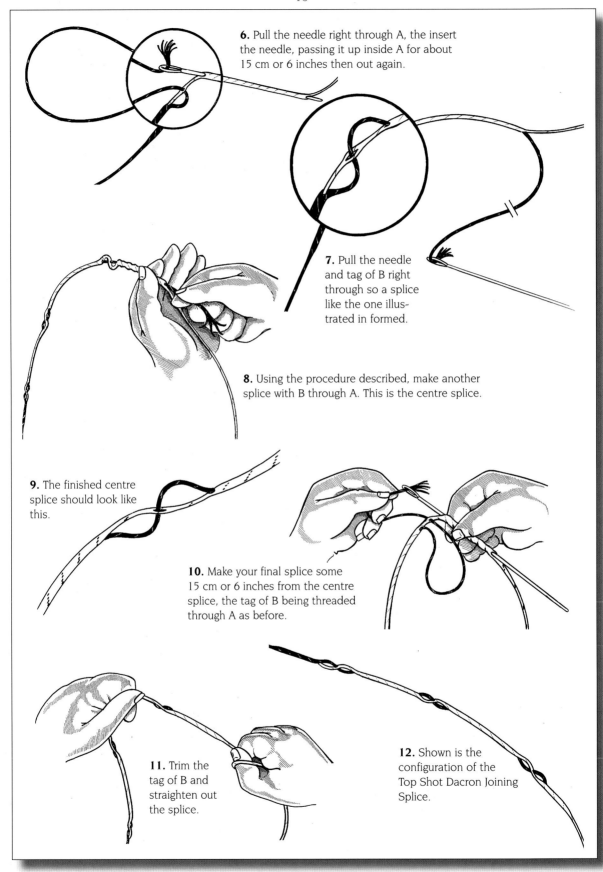

6. Pull the needle right through A, the insert the needle, passing it up inside A for about 15 cm or 6 inches then out again.

7. Pull the needle and tag of B right through so a splice like the one illustrated in formed.

8. Using the procedure described, make another splice with B through A. This is the centre splice.

9. The finished centre splice should look like this.

10. Make your final splice some 15 cm or 6 inches from the centre splice, the tag of B being threaded through A as before.

11. Trim the tag of B and straighten out the splice.

12. Shown is the configuration of the Top Shot Dacron Joining Splice.

DACRON LEADER SPLICE

Hollow braided lines permit heavy monofilament wind-on leaders to be attached without the use of knots by using the following procedure.

1. Take the required length of monofilament leader testing twice to four times the breaking strain of the hollow dacron line on your reel and shave it to a taper at one end.

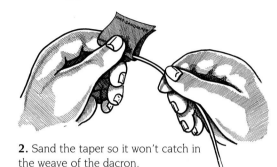

2. Sand the taper so it won't catch in the weave of the dacron.

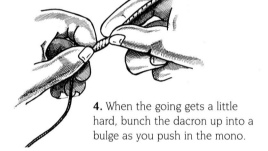

3. Feed the heavy monofilament leader inside the dacron.

4. When the going gets a little hard, bunch the dacron up into a bulge as you push in the mono.

5. Pinch the leader and smooth the bulge back toward the start. This will help you to keep working the heavy mono leader further into the dacron.

6. After you have worked the monofilament 30 cm (12 inches or so), into the dacron, you will find it impossible to pull the monofilament out. At this point, however, the dacron may be pushed off the monofilament quite easily just by sliding your fingers up against it.

7. To secure the splice, we make a firm lashing of half hitches on the dacron/mono join with the some waxed thread or like, beginning with a clove hitch on the mono, just below the dacron end, working up over the join in the same manner as we finished off the Top Shot wind on leader on page 36. The binding is covered with at least one coat of a pliable, waterproof sealing agent like Aquaseal or Pliobond and allowed to dry before use.

SHIGESHI TANAKA'S LOOP

This method of splicing a loop in dacron, heavy gelspun or other hollow braided leader material, was created by well known stand-up game fisherman, Shigeshi Tanaka of Japan.
This loop is totally secure with no movement at all making it ideal for the Cat's Paw, and similar connections used with wind-on leaders. It is best performed using a Top Shot dacron loop-splicing needle made by Top Shot Tackle Australia.

1. Select a length of dacron or other hollow braided line of suitable diameter for the wind-on leader you intend building. Pass the loop splicing needle through the weave, more or less at right angles, about one third the way along, and thread the needle with the short end tag.

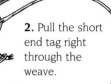

2. Pull the short end tag right through the weave.

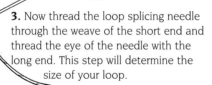

3. Now thread the loop splicing needle through the weave of the short end and thread the eye of the needle with the long end. This step will determine the size of your loop.

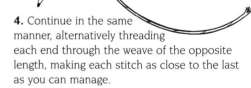

4. Continue in the same manner, alternatively threading each end through the weave of the opposite length, making each stitch as close to the last as you can manage.

5. The splice may be finished off by simply trimming the short tag after the final stitch, or ...

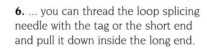

6. ... you can thread the loop splicing needle with the tag or the short end and pull it down inside the long end.

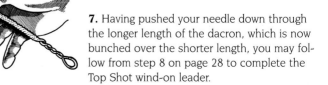

7. Having pushed your needle down through the longer length of the dacron, which is now bunched over the shorter length, you may follow from step 8 on page 28 to complete the Top Shot wind-on leader.

KNOT TEST ON GELSPUN FISHING LINE

The objects of these tests were to discover the true strength of a number of gelspun lines submitted for test and how much of that strength could be retained by using various knots, joins and splices.

FUSION—A LINE BY SPIDERWIRE LABELLED AS 24 POUND B/S

TEST 1
Bimini Double tied to hook using a Silly Snell.
A Bimini double was tied in the end of the Fusion sample, then—using the double strand produced—a Silly Snell, was used to tie on a size 6/0 hook.

The line broke on the spool at a reading of 11.5 kg (25.3 lbs), about 5% higher than the breaking strain stated on the spool.

TEST 2
Plaited Double tied to 6/0 hook with Silly Snell.
The line broke between plait and spool at 12.4 kg, 14% above the line's stated breaking strain.

TEST 3
Spider Hitch Double tied to 6/0 with Silly Snell.
Spider Hitch broke at 7.2 kg (15.8 lbs), 79% of line's stated breaking strain.

TEST 4
Single strand of Fusion tied to hook using a Braid Snell.
A size 6/0 hook was attached to a single strand of Fusion using a Braid Snell. The snell broke at 11.4 kg, retaining 105% of the line's stated breaking strain.

TEST 5
Single strand of Fusion tied to the eye of a 6/0 hook using a Collar and Capstan.
This knot broke at 10 kg, (22 lbs) or approximately 92% of the line's stated breaking strain.

TEST 6
Palomar Knot.
A single strand of Fusion was tied to the eye of a size 6/0 hook using a Palomar Knot. The knot broke at 7.5 kg (16.5 lbs) or 69% of the stated breaking strain of the line.

TEST 7
Triple Palomar Knot.
A single strand of Fusion was tied to the eye of a 6/0 hook using a Triple Palomar Knot. The knot broke at 8.9 kg (19.6 lbs) retaining 82% of the line's stated breaking strain.

TEST 8
Braid Ring Knot.
Same result using the Braid Ring Knot as the Triple Palomar, retaining 82% of the line's stated breaking strain.

TEST 9
Joining two lines using a Blood Knot.
Although the blood knot is useful for joining monofilament, it was a failure in Fusion, breaking at 4.4 kg (9.6 lbs), retaining only 40% of the Line's stated breaking strain.

The results of the blood knot test are deleted from the other products because of similar or worse performance.

TEST 10
Opposed Nail Knot.
Although useful in monofilament, the Opposed Nail Knot broke at 6.5 kg (14.3 lbs) in the Fusion sample, retaining only 60% of the line's stated breaking strain.

As opposed nail knot's performance was worse in other lines results have been deleted.

TEST 11
Two Bimini Doubles joined with a Cat's Paw. (Bimini Cat's Paw Splice).
This test involved tying a short Bimini Double in the end of each line to be joined, then— using the loop-to-loop connection called a Cat's Paw—the doubles were joined.

The join between the two lines remained intact while the braid snell on the hook broke at 11.3 kg (25 lbs) or about 104% of the line's stated breaking strain.

The hook was then attached the remainder of line using another braid snell. The braid snell again broke, this time at a surprising 12.1 kg or 11% more than the stated breaking strain of the line.

The Cat's Paw join survived two tests of the most severe type without breaking, but became bunched very tightly and the line became discoloured (pale) each side of the join.

TEST 11A
Given the unexpectedly high result of Test 11, it was repeated with fresh line and an extra Bimini Double tied to a hook with a Silly Snell to engage the scales. This time the line broke at 12.4 kg outside of the join, 14% over the line's stated breaking strain.

TEST 12
Bimini Double in Fusion to 60 pound monofilament (Jinkai) leader using the Braid Leader Knot.
A Bimini Double was tied in the Fusion and attached to a length of 60 pound monofilament using the Braid Leader Knot.

All knots remained intact and the Fusion broke at 12.4 kg between spool and Bimini some 14% above the stated breaking strain.

CONCLUSIONS:
The sample of Fusion tested appeared to be 14% stronger than labelled; 12.4 kg (27.3 lbs). It was also found that Fusion can be rigged for fishing with no significant loss of breaking strain provided the correct knots are used.

RECOMMENDED KNOTS
* Joining two separate lengths of line:
Double Bimini to Cat's Paw with ten folds.

* Attaching a heavier monofilament leader for sport-fishing, lure-casting or bottom-bouncing in deep water:
Short Bimini Double to Braid Leader Knot. Plaited Double to Braid Leader Knot.

* Attaching a hook directly to Fusion:
Braid Snell.

* Attaching a lure directly to Fusion:
Collar and Capstan.

PLATYPUS 20 POUND SUPER BRAID

TEST 1
Bimini Double tied to a 6/0 hook with Silly Snell.
Line parted between spool and Bimini at 9.9 kg (21.8 lbs) 109% of the line's breaking strain.

TEST 2
Plaited Double.
Plait broke at 9 kg (19.8 lbs), 99% of the line's stated breaking point.

TEST 3
Spider Hitch.
Spider Hitch broke at 4.9 kg (10.7 lbs) 48.5% of the line's stated breaking strain.

TEST 4
Single strand of line attached to hook with a Braid Snell.
This test was lower than expected at 7.6 kg. I repeated the test three more times and the results were 8.1 kg, 8.9 kg and 8.1 kg. The average overall was 8.2 kg (18 lbs), 90% of the line's stated breaking strain.

TEST 5
Collar and Capstan.
Knot broke at 6.7 kg (14.8 lbs) or 74% of lines stated breaking strain. Re-tied the same knot with six wraps around the eye with little improvement.

TEST 6
Palomar Knot.
Broke at 5.2 kg (11.46 lbs), 57% of the line's stated breaking point.

TEST 7
Triple Palomar Knot.
Broke at 8.5 kg (18.7 lbs), 93.5% of the line's stated breaking strain.

TEST 8
Braid Ring Knot.
Broke at 6.7 kg (16.75 lbs), 83.5% of the line's stated breaking strain.

TEST 9
Lines joined by tying a Bimini Double in each end and using the Cat's Paw loop to loop connection with ten folds.
Broke at 6.0 kg (13.2 lbs), 66.5% of line's stated breaking strain.

TEST 10
Lines joined by tying a Bimini Double in each end then tying a short length of 30 lb monofilament between the two Bimini Doubles with a Braid Leader Knot to each.
The join remained intact with one of the Biminis breaking at 9.4 kg (20.7 lbs), 103.5% of the line's stated breaking strain. The test was repeated with a similar result.

TEST 11
Bimini Double to 30 pound mono leader using a Braid Leader Knot.
Bimini Double failed at 9.2 kg (20.2 lbs), 101% of the line's stated breaking strain. This test was repeated several times with all results above the line's stated breaking strain.

CONCLUSIONS:
This line is probably 9% stronger than the 20 pounds breaking strain stated.

RECOMMENDED KNOTS
*Terminals:
Bimini or Plaited Double to all terminals.
*Single Strand connections:
Not recommended, but Triple Palomar produced the best result at 93% of the line's stated breaking strain.
*Joining two separate lengths of line:
Bimini or Plaited Double in the end of each line, joined to an inter-linking length of heavier monofilament with a Braid Leader Knot at each end.
*Attaching a heavier monofilament leader fir sport-fishing, lure-casting or bottom-bouncing in deep water:
Short Bimini Double to Braid Leader Knot. Plaited Double to Braid Leader Knot.

OPAL SOFT-WIRE 19 POUND B/S GELSPUN MONOFILAMENT LINE

TEST 1
Bimini Double tied to a 6/0 hook with Silly Snell.
Line parted between spool and Bimini at 9.9 kg (21.8 lbs) 109% of the line's stated breaking strain.

TEST 2
Plaited Double to Hook with Silly Snell.
Plait broke at 9 kg (19.8 lbs), 104% of the line's stated breaking strain.

TEST 3
Spider Hitch.
Spider Hitch broke at 5.7 kg (12.5 lbs), 66% of line's stated breaking strain.

TEST 4
Braid Snell.
Snell broke at 10.5 kg (23.2 lbs), 122% of the line's stated breaking strain.

TEST 5
Collar and Capstan.
Broke at 6.0 kg (13.2 lbs) or 70% of line's stated breaking strain.

TEST 6
Palomar Knot.
Broke at 6.5 kg (14.36 lbs), 76% of the line's stated breaking point.

TEST 7
Triple Palomar Knot.
Knot broke at 7.0 kg (15.4 lbs), 80% of the line's stated breaking strain.

TEST 8
Braid Ring Knot.
Knot broke at 8.8 kg (19.36 lbs), 102% of the line's stated breaking strain.

TEST 9
Lines joined by tying a Bimini in each end attached with the Cat's Paw loop-to-loop connection.
Cat's Paw broke at 10.6 kg (23.3 lbs), 123% of the line's stated breaking strain.

TEST 10
Braid Leader Knot to 30 l pound monofilament leader.
Braid Leader Knot broke at 9.0 kg (19.8 lbs), 114% of the line's stated breaking strain.

TEST 11
Braid Leader Knot variation.
The broken double from the previous test was re-tied to the 30 pound monofilament using a variation of the Braid Leader Knot for broken doubles.

The 30 pound monofilament broke at the knot where it was tied to the scales at 11.8 kg (26 lbs), 137% of the Opal line's breaking strain. The Opal line, Bimini and leader knot remained intact.

CONCLUSIONS:
This line would seem to be at least 37% stronger than stated.

RECOMMENDED KNOTS

*Terminals:
Terminal rigging should begin with a Bimini or Plaited Double.

*Single Strand connections:
Not recommended, but Braid Snell was the strongest single strand hook connection, the Braid Ring Knot gave the best results for tying on lures and making other ring connections using only a single strand of line.

20 POUND CORTLAND SPECTRON

TEST 1
Bimini Double to a 6/0 with Silly Snell.
Line broke on spool at 9.8 kg (21.6 lbs), 8% higher than the breaking strain stated on the spool.

TEST 2
Plaited Double.
Plait broke at 8 kg (17.6 lbs), 88% of the line's stated breaking strain.

TEST 3
Spider Hitch.
Spider Hitch broke at 4.7 kg (10.3 lbs), 51.5% of line's stated breaking strain.

TEST 4
Braid Snell.
The Braid Snell broke at 8.9 kg (19.6 lbs), 98% of the line's stated breaking strain.

TEST 5
Collar and Capstan.
The Collar and Capstan broke at 6.8 kg (15 lbs) or 75% of line's stated breaking strain.

TEST 6
Palomar Knot.
Palomar Knot broke at 4.7 kg (14.36 lbs), 76% of the line's stated breaking point.

TEST 7
Triple Palomar Knot.
The Triple Palomar knot broke at 5.75 kg (12.6 lbs), 63% of the line's stated breaking strain.

TEST 8
Braid Ring Knot.
Braid Ring Knot broke at 5.2 kg (11.5 lbs), 42% of the line's stated breaking strain.

TEST 9
Bimini Double to Braid Leader Knot and 30 pound monofilament leader.
Braid Leader Knot broke at 8.7 kg (19.2 lbs), 96% of the line's stated breaking strain.

TEST 10
Broken Double re-tied to 30 lb mono using the Braid Leader Knot variation.
Broke at 8.2 kg (18 lbs), 90% of the line's stated breaking strain.

TEST 11
Two separate lengths of line joined by tying a Bimini Double in each and joining them together with a ten-fold Cat's Paw.
Cat's Paw broke at 9.1 kg (20 lbs), 100% of the line's stated breaking strain.

CONCLUSIONS:
The actual breaking strain of this line is difficult to ascertain because all breakages were within knots, joins, splices or on the spool. The highest test recorded was 8% higher than the 20 pound stated on the spool.

RECOMMENDED KNOTS
*Terminals:
Bimini Double to all terminals.
*Joins:
Short Bimini Double to be tied in each end of line to be joined, then the doubles are interlocked with a ten-fold Cat's Paw.

30 POUND BERKLEY GORILLA BRAID

TEST 1
Bimini Double.
Line broke on spool at 14.8 kg (32.6 lbs), 108.5% of the line's stated breaking strain.

TEST 2
Plaited Double.
Plait broke at 13.9 kg (30.6 lbs), 102% of the line's stated breaking strain.

TEST 3
Spider Hitch.
Hitch broke at 6.2 kg (13.6 lbs), 45% of stated breaking strain.

TEST 4
Braid Snell.
Braid Snell broke at 14.8 kg (32.6 lbs), 108.5% of the line's stated breaking strain.

TEST 5
Collar and Capstan.
Collar and Capstan broke at 11.0 kg (24.2 lbs), or 76% of the line's stated breaking strain.

TEST 6
Palomar Knot.
Palomar broke at 9.0 kg (19.0 lbs), 66% of the line's stated breaking point.

TEST 7
Triple Palomar Knot.
Triple Palomar broke at 10.3 kg (22.7 lbs), 76% of the line's stated breaking strain.

TEST 8
Braid Ring Knot.
Braid Ring Knot broke at 9.95 kg (22 lbs), 73.5% of the line's stated breaking strain.

TEST 9
Bimini Double to Braid Leader Knot in 60 pound monofilament.
Braid Leader Knot broke at 13.0 kg (28.6 lbs), 95% of line's stated breaking strain.

TEST 10
Broken Double was re-tied to the 60 pound monofilament.
Knot broke at 13.9 kg (30.6 lbs), 102% of the line's stated breaking strain.

TEST 11
Separate lengths of line were joined by tying a Bimini Double in each and interlocking them with a ten-fold Cat's Paw.
Cat's Paw broke at 10.5 kg (23.1 lbs), 77% of line's stated breaking strain.

TEST 12
Separate lengths of line were joined by tying a Bimini Double in each and introducing a length of 60 pound monofilament as a joining with a Braid Leader Knot each end.
One Braid Leader Knot broke at 13.6 kg (30 lbs), 100% of line's stated breaking strain.

CONCLUSIONS:
The actual breaking strain of this line was hard to ascertain because all breaks were either in joins, knots, splices, or on the spool. However, two tests gave a reading 8.5% over the line's stated breaking strain.

RECOMMENDED KNOTS

*Terminals:
Bimini Double to all terminals.

*Single Strand connections to hook:
Braid Snell.

*Single Strand connections to lures:
Braid Ring Knot, Collar and Capstan or Triple Palomar.

*Joins:
Strongest join was obtained by tying Bimini Doubles in the ends to be joined and introducing a length of 60 pound momofilament with Braid Leader Knots at each end.

30 POUND SPIDERWIRE (SPECTRA 2000)

TEST 1
Bimini Double to Silly Snell.
Reached limit of scales at 15 kg, (33 lbs), 110% of line's stated breaking strain without breaking.

TEST 2
Plaited Double.
Plait broke at 12.0 kg (26.4 lbs), 88% of the line's stated breaking strain.

TEST 3
Spider Hitch.
Spider Hitch broke at 5.7 kg (12.5 lbs), 41.5% of line's stated breaking strain.

TEST 4
Braid Snell.
Braid Snell broke at 14.5 kg (32 lbs), 107% of the line's stated breaking strain.

TEST 5
Collar and Capstan.
Collar and Capstan broke at 11.8 kg (26 lbs), or 87% of the line's stated breaking strain.

TEST 6
Palomar Knot.
Palomar broke at 10.0 kg (22 lbs), 73.5% of the line's stated breaking strain.

TEST 7
Triple Palomar Knot.
Triple Palomar broke at 11.5 kg (25.3 lbs), 84% of the line's stated breaking strain.

TEST 8
Braid Ring Knot.
Braid Ring Knot broke at 11.5 kg (25.3 lbs), 84% of the line's stated breaking strain.

TEST 9
Bimini Double to Braid Leader Knot attaching 60 pound monofilament leader.
Braid Leader Knot broke at 15 kg (33 lbs), 110% of line's stated breaking strain.

TEST 10
Broken Double was re-tied to the 60 pound monofilament using the Braid Leader Knot variation.
Knot again broke at 15 kg.

TEST 11
Joining two separate lines with Bimini Double each end interlocked with a ten-fold Cat's Paw.
Cat's Paw broke at 12.5 kg (27.5 lbs), 91.5% of line's stated breaking strain.

CONCLUSION:
This line is at least 10% stronger than stated.

RECOMMENDED KNOTS

*Terminals:
Bimini Double to all terminals.

*Single Strand to hook:
Braid Snell.

*Single Strand to lure:
Collar and Capstan, Triple Palomar & Braid Ring Knot.

*Joins:
1. Bimini Double in each end to be joined to ten-fold Cat's Paw.
2. Bimini Double in each end to be joined with a short length of 60 pond monofilament tied each end with a Braid Leader Knot.

30 POUND SPIDERWIRE PREMIUM BRAID

TEST 1
Bimini Double tied to hook using a Silly Snell.
Line broke on spool at 13.4 kg (29.5 lbs), 98% of the line's stated breaking strain.

TEST 2
Plaited Double tied to hook with Silly Snell.
Line broke within plait at 12.1 kg (26.6 lbs), 89% of the line's stated breaking strain.

TEST 3
Spider Hitch double to hook with Silly Snell.
Line broke on the snell at 12.7 kg (28 lbs), 93% of the line's stated breaking strain.

TEST 4
Braid Snell.
Braid Snell broke at 14.5 kg (32 lbs), 107% of the line's stated breaking strain.

TEST 5
Silly Snell to hook (single strand).
Line broke on snell at 13.4 kg (29.5 lbs), 98% of the line's stated breaking strain

Given the unexpectedly high result with this knot the test was repeated. This time the snell broke at 11.1 kg (24.4 lbs), 81% of the line's stated breaking strain.

TEST 6
Collar and Capstan.
Line broke on the collar at 11.8 kg (26 lbs), 87% of the line's stated breaking strain.

TEST 7
Palomar Knot.
Knot broke at 8.1 kg (17.8 lbs), 59% of the line's stated breaking strain.

TEST 8
Triple Palomar Knot.
Knot broke at 11.6 kg (25.5 lbs), 85% of the line's stated breaking strain.

TEST 9
Braid Ring Knot.
Knot broke at 8.5 kg (18.7 lbs), 62% of the line's stated breaking strain.

TEST 10
Line doubled then tied to a hook with a six turn Uni Knot as recommended in the accompanying literature.
Knot broke at 10.4 kg (22.9 lbs), 76% of the line's stated breaking strain.

TEST 11
Two separate lines of line joined with opposed uni knots (double uni knot), as recommended in accompanying literature.
Double uni knot broke 6.3 kg (13.9 lbs), 46% of the line's stated breaking strain.
Given the low result of this test it was repeated. This time the double uni knot broke at 7.2 kg (15,8 lbs), 53% of the line's breaking strain.

TEST 12
Two separate lengths of line joined with a Bimini Cat's Paw splice.
The Cat's Paw failed at 13.4 kg (29.5 lbs), 98% of the line's stated breaking strain.

TEST 13
Bimini Double to Braid Leader Knot.
The line failed between the Bimini and the spool at 13 kg (30.6 lbs), 102% of the line's stated breaking strain.

CONCLUSION:
This line appears to be about 2% stronger than its stated breaking strain.

RECOMMENDED KNOTS
*Terminals:
Bimini Double usually produced the highest results.
*Single Strand to hook:
Braid Snell and Silly Snell.
*Joins:
Bimini Double in each end joined with a tenfold Cat's Paw.

SPIDERWIRE FUSION 14 POUND

TEST 1
Bimini Twist Double tied to a hook.
Line broke at 13.2 kg (29 lbs), 207% of the line's stated breaking strain.

TEST 2
Braid Snell tied to hook.
Line broke at 10.6 kg (23.3 lbs), 167% of the line's stated breaking strain, or about 80% of the line's probable breaking strain.

TEST 3
Double Uni Knot.
Two lengths were joined with 6 turn Double Uni Knots and tested until the join parted at 5.7 kg (12.5 lbs), 90% of the line's stated breaking strain, or about 43% of the Line's probable true breaking strain.

TEST 4
Bimini Cat's Paw Splice.
Two lengths were joined with a Bimini Cat's Paw Splice and tested until one Bimini parted at 10 kg (22 lbs), 157% of the line's stated breaking strain, or 76% of the line's probable true breaking strain. Test was repeated with the same result.

TEST 5
Albright Knot.
A length of bulk monofilament marked 50 pound breaking strain was attached using a 14 turn (seven turns in each direction) Albright Knot and tested until the Albright parted at 8.7 kg (19.2 lbs), 137% of the line's stated breaking strain or about 66% of the line's probable true breaking strain.

TEST 6
Braid Ring Knot.
A hook was attached using a Braid Ring Knot and tested till the knot parted at 8.9 kg (19.6 lbs), 140% of the line's stated breaking strain or about 68% of the line's probable true breaking strain.

TEST 7
Braid Leader Knot.
A length of bulk monofilament marked 30 pounds was attached by first tying a Bimini Twist Double and then a Braid Leader Knot which parted at 10.1 kg (22.2 lbs), 158% of the line's stated breaking strain or about 77% of the line's probable true breaking strain.

TEST 8
Mike Connolly's Leader Knot.
Mike Connolly's Leader Knot was tied to 35 lb monofilament with this line and the average of three breaks was 6.9 kg (15.2 lbs), 109% of the stated breaking strain or 52% of the probable true breaking strain.

FINS PRT BRAID 30 POUND (YELLOW)

TEST 1
Bimini Twist Double.
Bimini Twist Double was tied to a hook and tested until the line broke between the spool and hook at 17.5kg (38.5 lbs), about 129% of the lines stated breaking strain.

TEST 2
Braid Snell.
Braid Snell was tied to a hook and the break was measured at 16.5 kg (36.3 lbs), 121% of the line's stated breaking strain, or about 95% of the line's probable true breaking strain..

TEST 3
Double Uni Knot.
Two lengths were joined with 6 turn Double Uni Knots and tested until the join parted at 10.6 kg (23.3lbs), 78% of the line's stated breaking strain, or about 61% of the line's probable true breaking strain.

TEST 4
Bimini Cat's Paw Splice.
Two lengths of line were joined with a Bimini Cat's Paw Splice and tested until the line parted outside of all joins and splices at 17.5 kg, 129% of the line's stated breaking strain and 100% of the line's probable true breaking strain.

TEST 5
Albright Knot.
A length of bulk monofilament marked 50 pound breaking strain was attached using a 14 turn (seven turns in each direction) Albright Knot and tested until the Albright parted at 13.7 kg (30.1lbs), 100% of the line's stated breaking strain or 78% of the line's probable true breaking strain.

TEST 6
Silly Snell.
Line was tied to a hook using a Silly Snell and the break was measured at 8.3 kg (18.3 lbs), 28% of the line's stated breaking strain or 22% of the probable true breaking strain.

TEST 7
Braid Ring Knot.
A hook was attached using a Braid Ring Knot and tested till the knot parted at 13.9 kg (30.6lbs), 102% of the line's stated breaking strain or about 80% of the line's probable true breaking strain.

TEST 8
Braid Leader Knot.
A length of bulk monofilament marked 50 pounds was attached by first tying a Bimini Twist Double and then a Braid Leader Knot. The join parted at 17 kg (37.4 lbs); 124% of the lines stated breaking strain or 97% of the line's probable true breaking strain.

TEST 9
Mike Connolly's Leader Knot.
Mike Connolly's Leader Knot was tied to 35 lb monofilament with this line and the average of three breaks was 11.1 kg (24.5 lbs), 82% of the stated breaking strain or 64% of the probable true breaking strain.

SPIDERWIRE 30 POUNDS

TEST 1
Bimini Twist Double.
Bimini Twist Double was tied to a hook and tested until the Bimini broke at 26.5 kg (58.4lbs), 195% of the lines stated breaking strain.

TEST 2
Braid Snell.
Braid Snell was tied to a hook and the break was measured at 20 kg (44 lbs), 147% of the line's stated breaking strain, or about 75% of the line's probable breaking strain.

TEST 3
Double Uni Knot.
Two lengths were joined with 6 turn Double Uni Knots and tested until the join parted at 14.5 kg (32 lbs) 108% of the line's stated breaking strain, or about 55% of the line's probable breaking strain.

TEST 4
Bimini Cat's Paw Splice.
Two lengths of line were joined with a Bimini Cat's Paw Splice and tested until one Bimini parted at 25.5 kg (56.2 lbs), 187% of the line's stated breaking strain, or 97% of the line's probable breaking strain.

TEST 5
Albright Knot.
A length of bulk monofilament marked 50 pound breaking strain was attached using a 14 turn (seven turns in each direction) Albright Knot and tested until the Albright parted at 10 kg (22 lbs), 73% of the line's stated breaking strain or about 38% of the line's probable breaking strain. This test was repeated with the same unexpectedly low result.

TEST 6
Braid Ring Knot.
A hook was attached using a Braid Ring Knot and tested till the knot parted at 21.5 kg (47.4 lbs), 158 % of the line's stated breaking strain or about 81% of the line's probable true breaking strain.

TEST 7
Braid Leader Knot.
A length of 80 lb monofilament was attached by first tying a Bimini Twist Double and then a Braid Leader Knot which remained intact while the Bimini parted at 25.5 kg (56.2 lbs), 187% of the line's stated breaking strain, or 97% of the line's probable breaking strain.

TEST 8
Mike Connolly's Leader Knot.
Mike Connolly's knot was tied to 60 lb monofilament and tested five times. The average of those tests, which included two very low results, both at 9 kg was 12.06 kg or 26.5 lbs, 87% of the line's stated breaking strain or about 45% of the line's probable breaking strain.

Disregarding the two very low tests, the average was 14.1 kg (31 lbs), 104 % of the lines stated breaking strain or about 53% of the lines probable breaking strain.

GLUE TESTED ON KNOTS TIED IN GELSPUN FISHING LINE

The application of various glues to knots sometimes—but not always—has the effect of increasing the strength of the knot. Following are some tests carried out by the author on gelspun fishing lines to determine the effect of a cyanoacrylate glue marketed for this very purpose

TEST 1

A sample of Berkley Fireline, a fused, gelspun fishing line, marked 14 lbs—but with a true strength of more than twice this figure—was tied to a hook using a braid ring knot and tested. The knot broke at 7 kg (15.4 lbs).

The test was repeated after saturating the knot with glue. The result was the same with the knot breaking at 7 kg.

TEST 2

The 14 lb Berkley Fireline was tied to a hook using a braid snell and tested on the scales. The snell broke at 12.8kg (28.2 lbs).

The same test was repeated with the snell saturated with glue and allowed to dry. The snell broke at 10.8 kg (23.8 lbs). A reduction of 15% with the addition of the glue.

TEST 3

Two lengths of 14 lb Berkely Fireline were joined using a Bimini cat's paw splice with ten folds and the join tested. The cat's paw broke at 8.0 kg (17.6 lbs).

The test was repeated with the cat's paw saturated with glue then allowed to dry. The cat's paw broke at 7.1 kg, a reduction of 11%.

TEST 4

One of the remaining Bimini doubles was tied to a hook using a silly snell and tested. The 14 lb Berkley Fireline broke outside the Bimini at 13.2 kg (29 lbs).

With no apparent room for improvement there seemed no p[o]int in doing additional testing with the glue. However, I did test another Bimini after saturating it with the glue then allowing it to dry and got the same result.

TEST 5

A Bimini double was tied in a sample of Berkley Gorilla Braid marked 20 lb, but testing some 25% higher at 11.4 kg (25 lb). This in turn was tied to a hook with a silly snell and tested. The line broke on the spool at 11.4 kg.

The test was repeated with the Bimini twist saturated in glue and allowed to dry. The spool was wrapped in a handkerchief to minimise 'line bite' and the sample was tested. Once again the line broke outside the Bimini at 11.4 kg.

TEST 6

The 20 lb Berkley Gorilla Braid was tied to a hook using a braid ring knot with ten wraps and tested. The knot broke at 7.95 kg (17,5 lbs), 87% of the line's stated breaking strain or 70% of the line's actual breaking strain.

The same knot was tied, saturated with glue and tested when dry. The knot broke at 9.1 kg. 100% of the line's stated breaking strain or 80% of the line's actual breaking strain. An improvement of 15% or 10% in respect of the line's actual breaking strain.

TEST 7

Two separate lengths of line from the same spool of 20 lb Berkley Gorilla Braid

were joined with the Bimini cat's paw splice and tested. The cat's paw broke at 10.3 kg, 114% of the line's stated breaking strain or 90% of the line's actual breaking strain

The test was repeated with the cat's paw saturated with glue and allowed to dry. The cat's paw broke at 10.4 kg, a marginal improvement.

TEST 8

20 lb Berkely Gorilla Braid was tied to a loop of monofilament with an Albright knot producing two monofilament tags to which a hook and sinker could be tied (monofilament paternoster). The Albright knot failed at 4 kg, 45% of the line's stated breaking strain or 35% of the actual breaking strain.

The test was repeated after saturating the Albright knot with glue and allowing it to dry. This time the Albright knot failed at 5.7 kg, 63% of the line's stated breaking strain or 50% of the actaul breaking strain. An improvement of 40% or 15% in respect ot the line's breaking strain.

TEST 9

20 lb Berkely Gorilla Braid was tied to a hook with a Braid Snell and tested. The Braid Snell broke at 7.95 kg, 87% of the line's stated breaking strain or 70% of the actual breaking strain.

The test was repeated after the braid snell was retied, saturated with glue and allowed to dry. This time the braid snell broke at 10.6 kg, 117% of the line's stated breaking strain or 93% of the line"s actual breaking strain, an improvement of 33% or 23% in respect to the breaking strain of the line.

TEST 10

Two lengths of 20 lb Berkely Gorilla Braid were tied together with a double uni-knot

with four wraps on each side. The join began slipping undone when 3 kg (6.6 lbs) of tension was applied.

The same knot was tied, saturated with glue then tested. This time the double uni knot failed at 4.9 kg (10.8 lbs), indicating this knot is not suitable for joining gelspun fishing lines under any circumstances.

TEST 11

20 lb Berkely Gorilla Braid was tied to a using the 'Berkley Braid Knot' and tested. The knot failed at just under 5 kg (11.0 lbs). Considering this knot is described on the Berkley Gorilla Braid packet, and recommended for use with Berkley Gorilla Braid, the test was repeated twice, both times with the same poor result.

The knot was tied a fourth time and saturated with the glue. After the glue was allowed to dry, the test was repeated. This time the 'Berkley Braid Knot' broke at 9.9 kg (21.8 lbs) or 109% of the line's stated breaking strain, or 87% of the line's actual breaking strain.

TEST 12

In accordance with literature accompanying the glue, a knotless hook attachment was attempted with the 20 lb Gorilla Braid by threading the line into a 1 cm (app. 3/8") length of plastic tube with an I.D. of approximately 1 mm (3/64"). The join slipped undone under a strain of 4.0 kg.

The test was repeated using a much finer diameter plastic tube which could only be threaded with great difficulty. Again the join slipped undone under a strain of only 4 kg suggesting this join is unsuitable for gelspun fishing lines.

However this same knotless leader connection was successful with 30 lb dacron, testing at 13.0 kg (28.6 lbs).

CONCLUSION

Cyanoacrylate glue may be useful insurance against knot failure if the knots are poorly tied or poorly chosen. However, its application to the fused sample of gelspun line (14 lb Berkely Fireline) made little difference, in fact some tests indicated a reduction in strength following the application of the glue.

On the other hand, a significant improvement in knot strength was noticed in most cases when the glue was applied to knots tied in the braided gelspun line (Berkely Gorilla Braid). This was despite some of those knots testing quite high.